D0519131

Carpe Diem

make the most of life

summersdale

CARPE DIEM

Summersdale Publishers Ltd
46 West Street
Chichester
West Sussex
PO19 1RP
UK

www.summersdale.com

Printed and bound in the Czech Republic

ISBN: 978-1-84953-485-7

Substantial discounts on bulk quantities of Summersdale books are available to corporations, professional associations and other organisations. For details contact Nicky Douglas by telephone: +44 (0) 1243 756902, fax: +44 (0) 1243 786300 or email: nicky@summersdale.com.

To...........................

From...................

Carpe Diem

The envious moment is flying now,

now, while we're speaking:

Seize the day, place in the hours

that come as little faith as you can.

Horace

Open the curtains and let a new day begin!

With the new day
comes new strength
and new thoughts.

Eleanor Roosevelt

You are never too
old to set another
goal or to dream a
new dream.

C. S. Lewis

Be a child again today, and spread some mischief!

Act as if what
you do makes a
difference. It does.

William James

Opportunities
multiply as they
are seized.

Sun Tzu

Build something **today,** however small.

I'd rather regret
the things I've
done than regret
the things I
haven't done.

Lucille Ball

If you're going
through hell,
keep going.

Winston Churchill

Without obstacles, life would just be a race - and that wouldn't be half as much fun.

In the middle
of difficulty lies
opportunity.

Albert Einstein

One may walk
over the highest
mountain one step
at a time.

John Wanamaker

Share the fun **wherever** you go today.

Wherever you are
- be all there.

Jim Elliot

Things do not
happen. Things are
made to happen.

John F. Kennedy

Today is a blank page - what are you going to write on it?

Who seeks
shall find.

Sophocles

If you ask me what
I came into this life
to do, I will tell you:
I came to live
out loud.

Émile Zola

Good things
come to those who...
go out and
get them!

For myself, I am an optimist – it does not seem to be much use being anything else.

Winston Churchill

Whenever you fall,
pick something up.

Oswald Avery

Every change brings opportunity with it.

Either you run the
day or the day
runs you.

Jim Rohn

Tell me, what is it
you plan to do
with your one wild
and precious life?

Mary Oliver

Who cares about winning or losing? Life is about taking part.

Expect problems
and eat them
for breakfast.

Alfred A. Montapert

The most effective
way to do it,
is to do it.

Amelia Earhart

I can,
therefore
I am.

Simone Weil

In order to
succeed, we must
first believe that
we can.

Nikos Kazantzakis

You are the

hero

of your story.

You must be the change you wish to see in the world.

Mahatma Gandhi

Life is simple,
it's just not easy.

Anonymous

What are you waiting for?

Nothing really
matters except
what you do now in
this instant of time.

Eileen Caddy

No one knows what
he can do till
he tries.

Publilius Syrus

Make a wish...
then make it
come true!

Life is a shipwreck,
but we must not
forget to sing in
the lifeboats.

Voltaire

Whether you think
you can or you
think you can't,
you're right.

Henry Ford

Who's that in the mirror? Looks like a go-getter to me.

Life isn't about finding yourself. Life is about creating yourself.

George Bernard Shaw

Do what you can,
with what you have,
where you are.

Theodore Roosevelt

When life throws **tomatoes** at you, make a *Bloody Mary!*

When you reach the
end of your rope,
tie a knot in it and
hang on.

Thomas Jefferson

Perseverance is failing nineteen times and succeeding the twentieth.

Julie Andrews

You
only
live
once.

Opportunity
does not knock, it
presents itself when
you beat down
the door.

Kyle Chandler

Begin to be now
what you will be
hereafter.

William James

Squeeze
all the juice
out of today!

Set your goals high,
and don't stop till
you get there.

Bo Jackson

Nothing is a waste
of time if you use
the experience
wisely.

Auguste Rodin

Your life is a work of art -
it deserves to be seen.

Find ecstasy in life;
the mere sense of
living is joy enough.

Emily Dickinson

It's always too
early to quit.

Norman Vincent Peale

Don't race for the finish line - enjoy the journey.

If you wait, all that happens is that you get older.

Mario Andretti

One joy scatters a
hundred griefs.

Chinese proverb

Make
every minute
count.

How wonderful it
is that nobody
need wait a single
moment before
starting to improve
the world.

Anne Frank

It's OK to have butterflies in your stomach. Just get them to fly in formation.

Rob Gilbert

Grab a double helping of life, with a side order of adventure.

Life is either a
daring adventure
or nothing.

Helen Keller

Opportunities are
like sunrises. If you
wait too long, you
miss them.

William Arthur Ward

Life is sweet:
take a big bite!

There are always
flowers for those
who want to
see them.

Henri Matisse

You're the
blacksmith of your
own happiness.

Swedish proverb

To rest is to rust - stay shiny and **bright!**

We are all in the
gutter but some of
us are looking
at the stars.

Oscar Wilde

Some days there
won't be a song
in your heart.
Sing anyway.

Emory Austin

Sing a song, paint a picture... change the world.

Live your questions
now, and perhaps
even without
knowing it, you will
live along some
distant day into
your answers.

Rainer Maria Rilke

The secret of
getting ahead is
getting started.

Mark Twain

Every dawn is a new beginning, a time to start a **new story.**

Setting goals is the
first step in turning
the invisible into
the visible.

Tony Robbins

The wise does at
once what the fool
does at last.

Baltasar Gracián

Why watch TV when *real life* is so much more *exciting?*

You can't use up
creativity. The more
you use, the more
you have.

Maya Angelou

Live today for
tomorrow it will all
be history.

Proverb

It is never too late
to be what you
might have been.

George Eliot

A journey of a
thousand miles
begins with a
single step.

Lao Tzu

Live life off the map and be your own compass.

The best way to
predict the future
is to create it.

Abraham Lincoln

Every artist was
first an amateur.

Ralph Waldo Emerson

Talk to someone new. You could make **their day** - and they might **make yours.**

I have never met
a man so ignorant
that I couldn't learn
something from him.

Galileo Galilei

To me, every hour of
the day and night
is an unspeakably
perfect miracle.

Walt Whitman

You are a song
- make sure
you're heard.

Life shrinks
or expands in
proportion to
one's courage.

Anaïs Nin

The best way to
make your dreams
come true is to
wake up.

Paul Valéry

Look at life from **unexpected** angles today.

To succeed in life,
you need three
things: a wishbone,
a backbone and
a funny bone.

Reba McEntire

Stand up and walk
out of your history.

Phil McGraw

Be who you've *always* wanted to be.

Look at life through
the windshield, not
the rear-view mirror.

Byrd Baggett

The best way out is
always through.

Robert Frost

Make your own sunshine.

Look at everything
as though you were
seeing it for the first
or last time.

Betty Smith

The man who removes a mountain begins by carrying away small stones.

Chinese proverb

You can do it.
All you have
to do is
try.

All life is an experiment. The more experiments you make, the better.

Ralph Waldo Emerson

If your ship
doesn't come in,
swim out to it.

Jonathan Winters

Just be
yourself.

There are exactly
as many special
occasions in life
as we choose
to celebrate.

Robert Brault

Life begins at
the end of your
comfort zone.

Neale Donald Walsch

life is not
a rehearsal
- enjoy the limelight!

Most folks are as happy as they make up their minds to be.

Abraham Lincoln

I have found that
if you love life,
life will love
you back.

Arthur Rubenstein

Enjoy today, don't worry about tomorrow.

If you're already
walking on thin ice,
you might as
well dance.

Proverb

I couldn't wait for
success, so I went
ahead without it.

Jonathan Winters

Go and get it!

You can have
anything you want
if you will give up
the belief that you
can't have it.

Robert Anthony

If the wind
will not serve,
take to the oars.

Latin proverb

Nobody can hold you back.

You can't expect
to hit the jackpot
if you don't put
a few nickels in
the machine.

Flip Wilson

Change your
life today. Don't
gamble on the
future, act now,
without delay.

Simone de Beauvoir

Show the world what you're made of.

Life isn't about waiting for the storm to pass; it's about learning to dance in the rain.

Anonymous

Shoot for the moon.
Even if you miss,
you'll land
among the stars.

Les Brown

Dress to impress and be the best you can be.

Don't get your
knickers in a knot.
Nothing is solved
and it just makes
you walk funny.

Kathryn Carpenter

Happiness is a way
of travel, not a
destination.

Roy M. Goodman

You're never lost - you're just discovering new places.

Opportunity is missed by most people because it is dressed in overalls and looks like work.

Thomas Edison

Difficulties
strengthen the
mind, as labour
does the body.

Seneca the Younger

Turn your hopes into realities.

Our greatest glory
is not in never
falling, but in rising
every time we fall.

Confucius

First say to yourself
what you would be;
and then do what
you have to do.

Epictetus

Make an
impression!

Luck is a dividend of sweat. The more you sweat, the luckier you get.

Ray Kroc

You can't wait for
inspiration. You
have to go after
it with a club.

Jack London

Welcome today's challenge.

When you come
to a roadblock,
take a detour.

Mary Kay Ash

The season of failure is the best time for sowing the seeds of success.

Paramahansa Yogananda

Spot the flowers that
grow up
through the cracks.

It's never too late
– never too late to
start over, never
too late to
be happy.

Jane Fonda

When it is darkest,
men see the stars.

Ralph Waldo Emerson

Be a gift to the world today.

You can't turn back
the clock but you
can wind it
up again.

Bonnie Prudden

The purpose of
our lives is to
be happy.

Dalai Lama

Doors are made to be opened; locks are made to fit a key.

What matters is to live in the present, live now, for every moment is now.

Sathya Sai Baba

Whoever is happy
will make others
happy too.

Anne Frank

Make new connections today!

A mind is like a
parachute. It
doesn't work if it
is not open.

Frank Zappa

With the past, I
have nothing to do;
nor with the future.
I live now.

Ralph Waldo Emerson